hen

butterflies

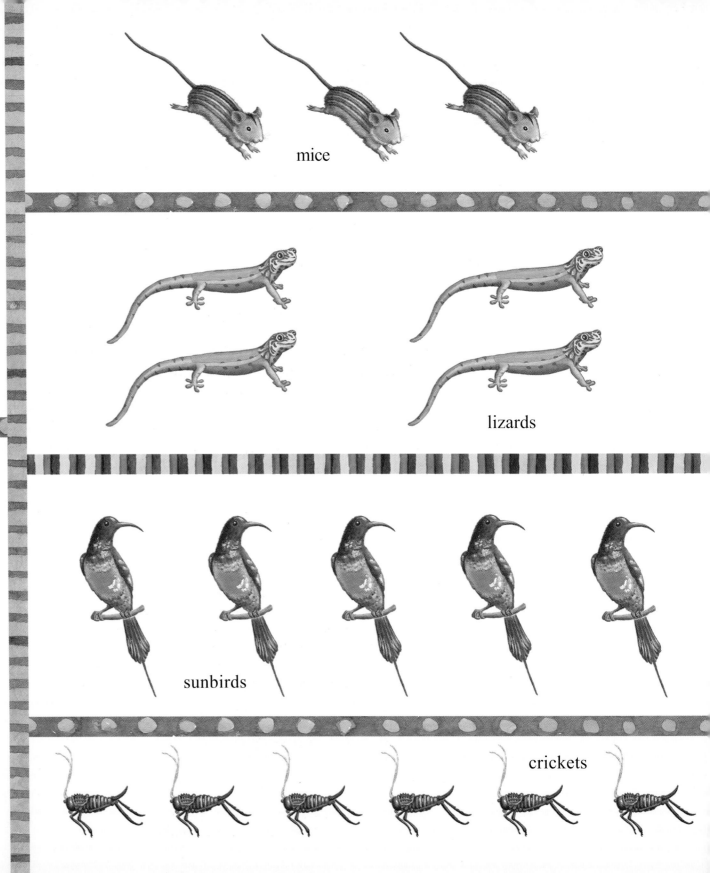

mice

lizards

sunbirds

crickets

baby bullfrogs

spoonbills

starlings

For John and Milo

The children featured in this book are from the Luo tribe of south-west Kenya.

*The wild creatures are the Citrus Swallowtail (butterfly), Striped Grass Mouse,
Yellow-headed Dwarf Gecko, Beautiful Sunbird, Armoured Ground Cricket,
(young) African Bullfrog, African Spoonbill and Superb Starling.*

*The author would like to thank everyone who helped her research this book,
in particular Joseph Ngetich from the Agricultural Office of the Kenya High Commission.*

Text and illustrations copyright © 2002 Eileen Browne
Dual Language copyright © 2003 Mantra Lingua
This edition published 2003
Published by arrangement with Walker Books Limited
London SE11 5HJ

British Library Cataloguing in Publication Data:
a catalogue record for this book is available from the British Library.

Published by
Mantra Lingua
5 Alexandra Grove, London N12 8NU
www.mantralingua.com

La Gallina di Handa

Handa's Hen

Eileen Browne

Italian translation by Paola Antonioni

mantra

La nonna di Handa ebbe una gallina nera.
Si chiamò Mondi – e ogni mattina
Handa diede colazione a Mondi.

Handa's grandma had one black hen.
Her name was Mondi - and every morning
Handa gave Mondi her breakfast.

Un giorno Mondi non arrivò a mangiare.
"Nonna!" disse Handa. "Hai visto Mondi?"
"No," disse la nonna "però vedo il tuo amico."
"Akeyo!" disse Handa. "Aiutami a trovare Mondi."

One day, Mondi didn't come for her food. "Grandma!" called Handa. "Can you see Mondi?"
"No," said Grandma. "But I can see your friend."
"Akeyo!" said Handa. "Help me find Mondi."

Mondi e Akeyo cercarono attorno al pollaio.
"Guarda, due farfalle svolazzanti," disse Akeyo.
"Ma dov'è Mondi?" disse Handa.

Handa and Akeyo hunted round the hen house.
"Look! Two fluttery butterflies," said Akeyo.
"But where's Mondi?" said Handa.

Guardarono attentamente sotto il deposito del grano.
"Shhh! Tre topi rigati," disse Akeyo.
"Ma dov'è Mondi?" disse Handa.

They peered under a grain store.
"Shh! Three stripy mice," said Akeyo.
"But where's Mondi?" said Handa.

Guardarono sotto i vasi di terracotta.
"Io vedo quattro piccole lucertole," disse Akeyo.
"Ma dov'è Mondi?" disse Handa.

They peeped behind some clay pots.
"I can see four little lizards," said Akeyo.
"But where's Mondi?" said Handa.

Cercarono attorno ad alcuni alberi fioriti.
"Cinque bellissimi uccelli da sole," disse Akeyo.
"Ma dov'è Mondi?" disse Handa.

They searched round some flowering trees.
"Five beautiful sunbirds," said Akeyo.
"But where's Mondi?" said Handa.

Guardarono nell' erba lunga e ondeggiante.
"Sei grilli saltanti!" disse Akeyo. "Prendiamoli."
"Voglio trovare Mondi," disse Handa.

The looked in the long, waving grass.
"Six jumpy crickets!" said Akeyo. "Let's catch them."
"I want to find Mondi," said Handa.

Andarono fino all' abbeveratoio.
"Piccole rane giganti," disse Akeyo. "C'è ne sono sette!"

They went all the way down to the water hole.
"Baby bullfrogs," said Akeyo. "There are seven!"

"Ma dov'è … oh guarda! Orme!" disse Handa.
Seguirono le orme e trovarono …

"But where's … oh look! Footprints!" said Handa.
They followed the footprints and found …

"Solo spatole," disse Handa. "Sette … no, otto.
Ma dov'è, oh dov'è Mondi?"

"Only spoonbills," said Handa. "Seven … no, eight.
But where, oh where is Mondi?"

"Spero che non sia stata mangiata da una spatola -
O mangiata da un leone," disse Akeyo.

"I hope she hasn't been swallowed by a spoonbill -
or eaten by a lion," said Akeyo.

Sentendosi tristi, tornarono verso la casa della nonna.
"Nove storni lucidi – la!" disse Akeyo.

Feeling sad, they went back towards Grandma's.
"Nine shiny starlings - over there!" said Akeyo.

"Ascolta," disse Handa. ^{pii} _{pii} "Quello cos'è?"

^{pii} _{pii} ^{pii} _{pii} ^{pii} _{pii} ^{pii} _{pii}

"Viene da sotto quel cespuglio. Ci guardiamo?"

"Listen," said Handa. ^{cheep} _{cheep} "What's that?"

^{cheep} _{cheep} ^{cheep} _{cheep} ^{cheep} _{cheep} ^{cheep} _{cheep}

"It's coming from under that bush. Shall we peep?"

Handa, Akeyo, Mondi e dieci pulcini

Handa, Akeyo, Mondi and ten chicks

corsero e saltarono fino alla casa della nonna ...

hurried and scurried and skipped back to Grandma's ...

dove fecero tutti colazione, molto tardi.

where they all had a very late breakfast.

hen

butterflies

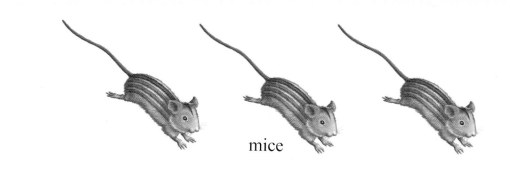

mice

lizards

sunbirds

crickets

baby bullfrogs

spoonbills

starlings

chicks